PORTRAITS OF THE STATES

VIRGINIA

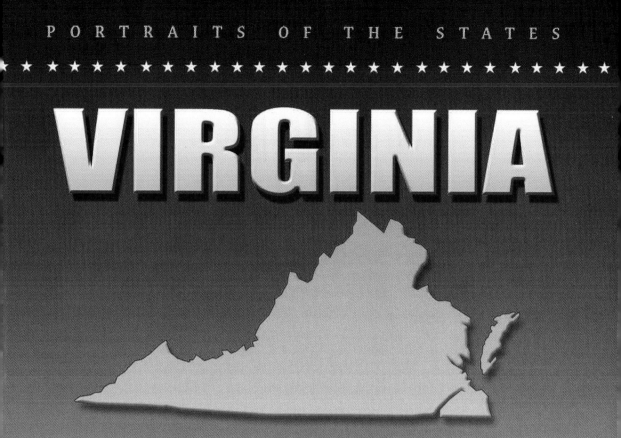

by Muriel L. Dubois

GARETH**STEVENS**

PUBLISHING

A Member of the WRC Media Family of Companies

Please visit our web site at: www.garethstevens.com
For a free color catalog describing Gareth Stevens Publishing's
list of high-quality books and multimedia programs, call
1-800-542-2595 (USA) or 1-800-387-3178 (Canada).
Gareth Stevens Publishing's fax: (414) 332-3567.

Library of Congress Cataloging-in-Publication Data

Dubois, Muriel L.
    Virginia / Muriel L. Dubois.
       p. cm. — (Portraits of the states)
    Includes bibliographical references and index.
    ISBN 0-8368-4636-2 (lib. bdg.)
    ISBN 0-8368-4655-9 (softcover)
    1. Virginia—Juvenile literature. I. Title. II. Series.
    F226.3.D83   2005
    975.5—dc22   2005042613

This edition first published in 2006 by
Gareth Stevens Publishing
A Member of the WRC Media Family of Companies
330 West Olive Street, Suite 100
Milwaukee, WI 53212 USA

This edition copyright © 2006 by Gareth Stevens, Inc.

Editorial direction: Mark J. Sachner
Project manager: Jonatha A. Brown
Editor: Betsy Rasmussen
Art direction and design: Tammy West
Picture research: Diane Laska-Swanke
Indexer: Walter Kronenberg
Production: Jessica Morris and Robert Kraus

Picture credits: Cover, pp. 25, 26 © Gibson Stock Photography; p. 4
© USAF/Getty Images; pp. 5, 8, 27 © Corel; p. 6 © Art Today; p. 11
© Library of Congress; p. 12 © Cynthia Johnson/Time & Life Pictures/Getty
Images; pp. 15, 21, 24 © PhotoDisc; p. 17 © MPI/Getty Images; p. 22
© Brian Fleske/U.S. Navy/Getty Images; p. 28 © Doug Pensinger/Getty Images

Printed in the United States of America

1 2 3 4 5 6 7 8 9 09 08 07 06 05

CONTENTS

Words that are defined in the Glossary appear
in **bold** the first time they are used in the text.

On the Cover: Virginia Beach is a great place to cool off on a
hot summer day.

Introduction

Virginia is a state that is full of history. Native Americans lived there long ago. Then, British men and women made it their home. Later, two wars were fought in Virginia's woods and fields.

Today, Virginia is a fun and interesting place to visit. You can travel on cool mountain roads or watch wild ponies run on a beach. In the cities, you can go to museums or visit theme parks. You can also visit the homes of some of the nation's early leaders. Welcome to Virginia.

The Pentagon in Arlington is the home of the U.S. Department of Defense. It is the biggest office building in the nation.

The state flag of Virginia.

VIRGINIA FACTS

- Became the 10th state: June 25, 1788
- Population (2004): 7,459,827
- Capital: Richmond
- Biggest Cities: Virginia Beach, Norfolk, Chesapeake, Richmond
- Size: 39,594 square miles (102,548 square kilometers)
- Nickname: The Old Dominion
- State Tree: American dogwood
- State Flower: American dogwood blossom
- State Bird: Cardinal
- State Insect: Tiger swallowtail butterfly
- State Dog: American foxhound

History

Virginia's first people were Native Americans. They hunted animals for food. They gathered plants to eat, too. Later, they planted corn, squash, and beans.

Settlers Arrive

In 1607, a group of British men sailed to the coast of Virginia. They built a **fort** at Jamestown. It was the first lasting European settlement in North America.

Many of the first white settlers got sick and died. Most of those who were left were not good hunters or farmers. Their leader, John Smith, began trading with the

This picture shows the wedding of John Rolfe and Pocahontas, a Native woman.

Natives for food. The food helped the settlers to survive.

More ships arrived. They brought people and supplies. One newcomer, John Rolfe, began planting tobacco. After he sold the leaves to Britain, other settlers planted tobacco, too. They became farmers.

In 1619, a Dutch ship arrived with twenty Africans on board. They were the first black slaves in North America. They worked on the farms.

Wars and Freedom

In 1624, Virginia became a **colony** and was ruled by Britain. Other colonies sprang up along the coast. Both France and Britain wanted to control them. The two countries fought over the colonies. In 1763, the British won the war.

Britain needed to pay for the war, so the king ruled that the colonies would pay **taxes**. Some colonists did not think the taxes were fair. Patrick Henry was one of them. He said Virginia should break away from Britain. He said, "Give me **liberty** or give me death!"

In 1775, the colonists began to fight for their freedom. This war was the Revolutionary War. Many people from Virginia fought

This painting shows the British surrendering to General George Washington in Yorktown.

in the war. George Washington led the army. Thomas Jefferson wrote the Declaration of Independence. It explained why the colonists wanted to be free.

The colonies wrote their own laws. They called themselves states. Virginia called itself a state in 1776.

The last big battle of the war was fought in Yorktown in 1781. The colonists won this battle and won the war.

Leaders from the old colonies got together and wrote laws for a new country. James Madison and George Mason of Virginia were part of this group. They helped write the U.S. Constitution. One by one, the states joined the new country. In 1788, Virginia was the tenth state to join the United States.

Problems over Slavery

By the 1800s, thousands of slaves lived in Virginia. They worked on large farms

FUN FACTS

Presidents from Virginia

In 1789, George Washington became the first president of the United States. Eight other U.S. presidents were also born in Virginia. More presidents have come from this state than from any other.

called plantations. Northern states did not have many large farms, and they did not need slaves. Slavery ended in the North. Many people in the North wanted slavery to end in the South, too. This idea was called **abolition**.

Southern states wanted to keep their slaves. They decided to break away from the northern states. Virginia and the other southern states formed the Confederate

States of America. Richmond became their capital.

Abraham Lincoln was the U.S. president at the time. He did not want the country to split in two. In 1861, his army began fighting to make the South come back to the **Union**. This was the start of the Civil War.

War and Ruin

Robert E. Lee of Virginia led the Confederate army. Lee

IN VIRGINIA'S HISTORY

Nat Turner's Rebellion

Nat Turner was a slave. In 1831, he led other slaves in an uprising against their white owners. This uprising took place in South Hampton County. The slaves killed fifty-eight white people. Turner and many others were caught and hanged. White people in the area were so angry that they killed many other slaves, too. These poor slaves had nothing to do with the uprising.

Famous People of Virginia

Booker T. Washington

Born: April 5, 1856, Franklin County, Virginia

Died: November 14, 1915, Tuskegee, Alabama

Booker T. Washington was born a slave. After the Civil War, he worked in coal mines. Then, he went to a school for blacks and worked as a janitor to pay his way. In 1881, he founded the Tuskegee Institute in Alabama to train black teachers. He worked hard to make the lives of African Americans better.

FUN FACTS

The U.S.S. *Monitor* and the C.S.S. *Virginia*

For hundreds of years, ships were built of wood. Cannons could easily blow big holes in these ships. The ships could catch on fire. By the time of the Civil War, ships were being built with iron sides. They were much sturdier. The first battle between ships with iron sides took place in Virginia. In 1862, the U.S.S. *Monitor* fought the C.S.S. *Virginia*. The battle lasted for four hours, and the ships were not damaged. Both sides claimed to have won the battle.

and his men fought many battles in his home state.

The war lasted four years, and thousands of people died. In 1865, the Union won the war. The peace treaty was signed at Appomattox Courthouse in

Virginia. Virginia became part of the United States again.

Virginia's cities were ruined, and many of its people were

This old photograph shows Union soldiers at Appomattox Courthouse in April 1865.

dead. Most people had lost most of their money.

Unequal Rights

A U.S. law ended slavery. Still, many white people did not want blacks to be truly free. Virginia and other states passed **segregation** laws. These laws kept blacks apart from whites. Black people were not allowed in white-only parks, schools, hotels, or bathrooms. They had their own places, but they were never as good as the places the white people had.

In the first half of the 1900s, the country fought in two wars in Europe and other places overseas. These wars were World War I and World War II. Virginia built ships and made supplies for

IN VIRGINIA'S HISTORY

Helping the Freed Slaves
Most slaves could not read or write. After the war, the U.S. government set up the Freedmen's Bureau to run schools for African Americans.

L. Douglas Wilder became the first black governor in the country in 1990.

go to the same schools. Virginia did not agree. Some schools closed down rather than let black children attend. But the U.S. laws kept giving more and more **civil rights** to black people. Finally, the U.S. government forced Virginia to end segregation. Now black people have the same rights as white people.

Virginia in the News

On September 11, 2001, terrorists stole an airplane and crashed it into the Pentagon in Arlington. Many people there were injured or killed.

these wars. This demand for supplies created new jobs. Life grew better for whites, but it did not change much for blacks.

Equal Rights

In 1954, the U.S. Supreme Court said segregation had to stop. The Court said it was wrong to send white children to one school and black children to another. All kids should be able to

IN VIRGINIA'S HISTORY

First Black Governor

In 1990, Virginia elected a black governor. L. Douglas Wilder was not just the first black man to become governor of this state, he was also the first African American governor in the whole country.

★ ★ ★ Time Line ★ ★ ★

1607	The first British settlers move to Virginia's coast.
1612	John Rolfe begins growing tobacco for sale in Britain.
1619	The first slaves arrive in Virginia.
1624	Virginia becomes a British colony.
1775–1783	Colonists fight against Britain in the Revolutionary War.
1787	The U.S. Constitution is written.
1788	Virginia becomes the tenth state.
1831	Nat Turner leads a slave rebellion.
1861	The Civil War begins, and Virginia leaves the Union. Richmond becomes the capital of the Confederate states.
1870	Virginia returns to the Union.
1900	Virginia passes segregation laws.
1917	U.S. involvement in World War I begins.
1941	U.S. involvement in World War II begins.
1954	The U.S. Supreme Court ends school segregation. Virginia closes its public schools.
1990	L. Douglas Wilder is elected Virginia's first black governor.
2001	On September 11, terrorists steal a plane and crash it into the Pentagon in Arlington.

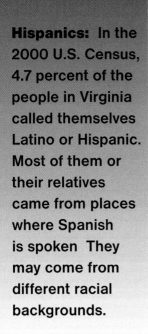

People

Native Americans were the first people to live in Virginia. Some were killed by guns brought by white settlers. Others died of diseases brought by the settlers. Most of those who were left were pushed out of the state. Few Natives still live in Virginia today.

In the 1600s, white colonists arrived from Britain. Although they struggled at first, their numbers grew. They became the largest group in the state. Today,

Hispanics: In the 2000 U.S. Census, 4.7 percent of the people in Virginia called themselves Latino or Hispanic. Most of them or their relatives came from places where Spanish is spoken They may come from different racial backgrounds.

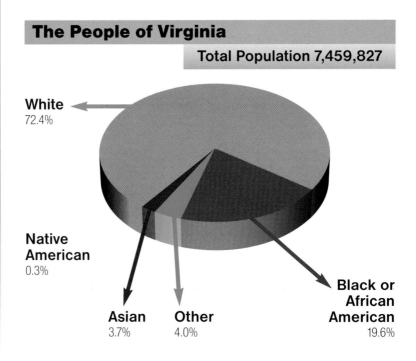

The People of Virginia

Total Population 7,459,827

White
72.4%

Native American
0.3%

Asian
3.7%

Other
4.0%

Black or African American
19.6%

Percentages are based on 2000 Census.

Richmond is the capital of Virginia and one of the biggest cities in the state.

about 70 percent of all Virginians are white.

Africans started coming to Virginia not long after the first white people. They were taken from their homes and carried off in chains. They came to Virginia as slaves. At one time, half of the state's people were black. After slavery ended, however, many African Americans left Virginia. They went north and west to find better lives. Today, about 20 percent of Virginians are black. Most of them live in cities. In some cities there, half the people are black.

Today, more than seven million people live in Virginia. Most make their homes in the eastern cities. Some of these cities have grown so much that they have spread into the countryside nearby. The eastern part of the state is

Famous People of Virginia

Thomas Jefferson

Born: April 13, 1743, Shadwell, Virginia

Died: July 4, 1826, Monticello, Virginia

Thomas Jefferson wrote the Declaration of Independence. Later, he became the third president of the United States. In between, he was Virginia's governor. He also made changes at William and Mary, the state's first college. He wanted the school to do more than train ministers. So students there began to study law, math, medicine, and other subjects. He also let the students choose the classes they wanted to take. No other college in the country had ever done this.

so full of people, buildings, and roads that it looks almost like one big city. The cities there just keep growing.

Churches and Schools

Most Virginians are Christians. Of these Christians, most belong to Protestant churches. There are some Catholics in the state, too, along with some Jews. Buddhists and Muslims also live in Virginia.

Virginia has not always had good schools. For many years, most white children were taught at home. The first public schools opened in 1846. At the time, only white children could go to these schools. Slave children were not allowed to go to school at all. After the Civil War, schools for African

Thomas Jefferson was one of the "founding fathers" of the United States. He was U.S. president from 1801 until 1809.

Famous People of Virginia

Ella Fitzgerald

Born: April 25, 1917, Newport News, Virginia

Died: June 15, 1996, Beverly Hills, California

An **orphan** at the age of fifteen, Ella Fitzgerald was placed in an orphanage for black children. Later, she ran away from a school she had been sent to. She was living in Harlem in New York when she sang in a contest at the Apollo Theater there. She won first place. She became a singer. Although she never received any real training, she went on to gain huge success as a singer. She became one of the most famous **jazz** singers in the world. She continued to perform until her death at the age of seventy-nine.

American children opened. Yet it was a very long time before black boys and girls could get an education as good as that of white children.

Virginia's first college, William and Mary, opened in 1693. Today, Virginia has many colleges, universities, and community colleges. The University of Virginia is one of the top schools in the nation.

The Land

The state of Virginia is shaped like a triangle and has three different **regions**. The Tidewater region is on the coast. The Piedmont area is in the middle. The mountains are in the west.

The Tidewater

The Tidewater is low and flat. This part of the state is filled with creeks, **swamps**, and rivers. Some of the rivers flow into the ocean. These rivers are called **estuaries**.

Most of the estuaries empty into the Chesapeake Bay on the Atlantic Ocean. The bay is long and narrow. It once was home to all kinds of fish and birds. But the land and water became badly **polluted**, or poisoned. Much of the wildlife in the area died. Today, people are taking better care of the bay, and the fish and birds are coming back again.

The Great Dismal Swamp is the biggest swamp in the Tidewater. Bald cypress and black gum trees grow in its flooded forests.

FUN FACTS

The Eastern Shore

One small part of Virginia is separate from the rest. This is the Eastern Shore. It is on the Delmarva **Peninsula**. This piece of land lies between the ocean and Chesapeake Bay. Some small islands are also part of the Eastern Shore.

The Eastern Shore has lots of wildlife. Sea turtles, dolphins, and whales swim in the waters off its coast. More than two hundred kinds of wild birds live on Assateague Island. This island is also home to wild ponies.

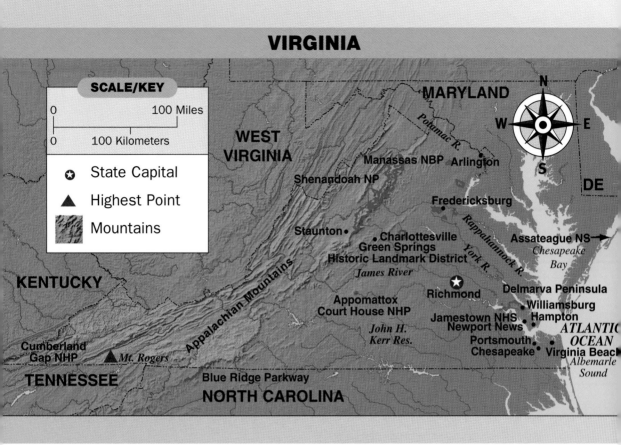

VIRGINIA

SCALE/KEY

0   100 Miles

0   100 Kilometers

⊛ State Capital

▲ Highest Point

Mountains

MARYLAND

WEST VIRGINIA

Potomac R.

Manassas NBP   Arlington

Shenandoah NP

Fredericksburg

DE

Rappahannock R.

Staunton

Charlottesville
Green Springs
Historic Landmark District

York R.

Assateague NS

Chesapeake Bay

KENTUCKY

James River

Appalachian Mountains

Appomattox
Court House NHP

Richmond

Delmarva Peninsula

Williamsburg

John H.
Kerr Res.

Jamestown NHS   Hampton
Newport News

ATLANTIC
OCEAN

Cumberland
Gap NHP

▲ Mt. Rogers

Portsmouth
Chesapeake

Virginia Beach

Albemarle
Sound

TENNESSEE

Blue Ridge Parkway

NORTH CAROLINA

People used to drain the swamps or fill them with soil because they wanted the land for farming. Today, the people of Virginia know that swamps are important homes for wildlife. They know that swamps keep larger bodies of water clean and prevent floods. Many are trying to protect what is left of Virginia's wetlands.

The Piedmont

The Piedmont is a land of rolling hills. Long ago, the colonists cut down trees so they could use the land for farming. Today, oak trees still grow in the area. Black gum, maple, and cypress trees grow along the rivers.

Many kinds of animals live in the Piedmont. Deer,

raccoons, and squirrels live there. Muskrats, beavers, and turtles are at home in the lakes and rivers.

The Mountains

Two mountain ranges rise up in the western part of the state. One is the Blue Ridge Mountains, and the other is the Appalachian Mountains. The Shenandoah River Valley lies between them.

Major Rivers

James River
340 miles (547 km) long

Potomac River
287 miles (462 km) long

Rappahannock River
212 miles (341 km) long

The mountains are covered with many kinds of trees. The state tree, the dogwood, blooms here in the spring. Black bears still live in this part of the state, along with deer, foxes, wild turkeys, quail, skunks, and chipmunks.

Virginia's highest point is Mount Rogers. This peak is 5,729 feet (1,746 meters) above sea level. This peak is in the Blue Ridge Mountains. Many caves stand near the Blue Ridge Mountains, too. Two of the most famous

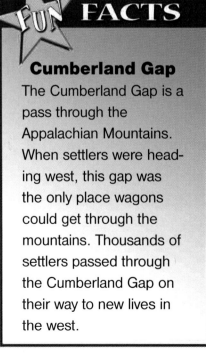

FUN FACTS

Cumberland Gap

The Cumberland Gap is a pass through the Appalachian Mountains. When settlers were heading west, this gap was the only place wagons could get through the mountains. Thousands of settlers passed through the Cumberland Gap on their way to new lives in the west.

caves are the Skyline and Luray **Caverns**.

Climate

Throughout the seasons, the state's climate remains mild. Springs are warm, while summers are hot and humid.

Natural Bridge is a famous sight in the Blue Ridge Mountains. Every year thousands of tourists come to these mountains to enjoy the lovely scenery.

Autumns get cool, and some snow falls in the winters.

Economy

Many people in Virginia have jobs with the U.S. government. Some of them work for the Pentagon in Arlington. Others work at the Marine Corps Base at Quantico.

The biggest navy base in the world is in Norfolk. It has many ships and provides jobs for thousands of people. Hampton Roads is not far away. It has a huge shipyard where ships are built and

This huge ship is one of many that has been repaired at the Norfolk Naval Shipyard.

repaired. Hampton Roads ships more coal than any other port in the world.

Many people in Virginia work in **tourism**. Visitors go to the state's parks, lakes, and national seashore. They go to museums and battle-fields. Workers in tourism sell tickets and give tours. They run hotels and work in restaurants.

Farming, Then and Now

Farming used to be a way of life for most people in Virginia. That is no longer so. Yet farmers on the Eastern Shore still grow potatoes, soybeans, and peanuts. Apples are a big crop in the Shenandoah River Valley. Farmers there raise hogs, beef cattle, dairy cattle, and turkeys.

How Money Is Made in Virginia

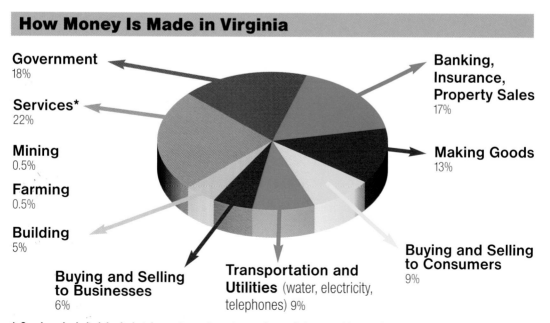

Government
18%

Services*
22%

Mining
0.5%

Farming
0.5%

Building
5%

Buying and Selling
to Businesses
6%

Transportation and
Utilities (water, electricity,
telephones) 9%

Buying and Selling
to Consumers
9%

Making Goods
13%

Banking,
Insurance,
Property Sales
17%

* Services include jobs in hotels, restaurants, auto repair, medicine, teaching, and entertainment.

Government

Richmond is the capital of Virginia. The leaders of the state work there. Virginia's government has three parts called branches. They are the executive, legislative, and judicial branches.

Executive Branch

The job of the executive branch is to carry out state laws. The governor leads this branch. He or she appoints many other state workers. The lieutenant governor helps the governor.

Thomas Jefferson designed the state capitol building in Richmond. He planned the building to look like a Roman temple.

The citizens of Virginia elect their governor and lieutenant governor. They also elect an attorney general.

Legislative Branch

Virginia's legislative branch is the General Assembly. It makes state laws. It also picks the judges for the state's courts. The General Assembly has two parts called houses. The Senate is one house. The House of Delegates is the other. The two houses work together.

Judicial Branch

The judicial branch **interprets** state laws. Judges hold court when people are **accused of** crimes. They make sure everyone accused of a crime gets a fair trial.

Mount Vernon was George Washington's home. Tourists now visit this historic home to see how wealthy people lived when the country was young.

VIRGINIA'S STATE GOVERNMENT

Executive		Legislative		Judicial	
Office	Length of Term	Body	Length of Term	Court	Length of Term
Governor	4 years	Senate (40 members)	4 years	Supreme (7 justices)	12 years
Lieutenant Governor	4 years	House of Delegates		Appeals (10 appeals)	8 years
		(100 members)	2 years		

25

Things to See and Do

Virginia has plenty of natural beauty. Many people like to swim at Virginia Beach. Others visit the wild ponies on Assateague Island. They watch birds, bike, swim, or collect seashells. Still others head west. They drive or hike through Shenandoah National Forest. They take tours through caves and see the strange rock forms inside.

History

Virginia has numerous historic places to visit. Fredericksburg, Yorktown, and other towns that saw Revolutionary and

Deep under the ground, the Luray Caverns contain many strange rock formations.

Old cannons stand guard on the grounds of Virginia Military Institute.

tours through the homes of George Washington and Thomas Jefferson. They visit Robert E. Lee's house, too.

Colonial Williamsburg is a living museum. Actors pretend to live there. They show visitors what life was like in the 1700s.

There is a living museum at Jamestown Settlement, too. It shows how the early settlers lived.

Civil War battles still honor their war heroes.

There are hundreds of museums and parks in the state. People often take

Famous People of Virginia

Edith Bolling Galt Wilson

Born: October 15, 1872, Whytheville, Virginia

Died: December 28, 1961, Washington, D.C.

Edith Bolling married President Woodrow Wilson in 1915. Four years later, the president had a stroke. He could not work, so Edith helped him. She sometimes was called "the secret president." People can learn more about her at the Wilson Presidential Library in Staunton.

Theme Parks

Virginia has great theme parks. Busch Gardens and Paramount's Kings Dominion are two of them. Visitors picnic, go on rides, and see shows at these parks. Many tourists head for water parks. There, they can swim, play in the water, and slide down water slides.

The Virginia Tech Hokies score a touchdown against the University of Pittsburgh Panthers.

Sports

College sports are popular in Virginia. Big crowds often turn out to watch football and basketball games.

Virginia also has some professional sports teams. All of these teams are in the minor leagues. The Richmond Braves are a baseball farm team for the Atlanta Braves.

FUN FACTS

Walton's Mountain

Virginia writer Earl Hamner Jr. is the creator of a television show called "The Waltons." Hamner based the fictional Walton family in the show on his own family. "The Waltons" was so popular that there is a Walton's Mountain Museum near Charlottesville. This museum recreates parts of the Waltons' house.

The Norfolk Tides are a farm team for the New York Mets.

The state also has minor league hockey. The Richmond Renegades won the 1994–1995 Riley Cup Championship.

The Softball Hall of Fame is in Petersburg. It honors the stars of the U.S. Slo-Pitch Softball Association. Richmond is home to the Round Robin Softball Tournament, one of the world's largest. The Virginia Sports Hall of Fame and Museum, in Portsmouth, honors state sports heroes.

Famous People of Virginia

Arthur Ashe

Born: July 10, 1943, Richmond, Virginia

Died: February 6, 1993, New York City, New York

Arthur Ashe was a great tennis player. In 1963, he played for the U.S. team in the Davis Cup tournament. He was the first African American to play for the team. Then, he was the top U.S. player in 1969. Six years later, he was ranked the number one tennis player in the world. Later, he worked for many good causes. In 1988, Ashe learned that he had HIV. He started a program to help others learn about HIV and AIDS.

★ ★

accused of — blamed for

abolition — putting an end to slavery

caverns — natural underground rooms and tunnels

civil rights — basic rights of a citizen, such as to vote, go to school, and own property

colony — a group of people living in a new land but controlled by the place they came from

estuaries — the parts of a river where it joins the sea

fort — a strong structure meant for protection

interprets — explains the meaning of something

jazz — a type of music started in the United States

liberty — freedom

orphan — a child whose parents have died

peninsula — a piece of land that is nearly surrounded by water

polluted — poisoned

regions — areas

segregation — separation from others based on skin color

swamps — wetlands, or areas that often flood, covered with trees, bushes, and grasses

taxes — money paid to the government

tourism — traveling for pleasure

Union — the United States of America

Books

Battle of Yorktown. Scott Ingram (Thomson Gale)

O Is for Old Dominion: A Virginia Alphabet. Pamela Duncan Edwards (Sleeping Bear Press)

Pocahontas: An American Princess. Joyce Milton (Grossett & Dunlap)

State Shapes: Virginia. Erik Bruun (Black Dog & Leventhal Publishers)

Virginia. State Books—from Sea to Shining Sea (series). Dennis Brindell Fradin (Children's Press)

Virginia Facts and Symbols. Bill McCauliffe (Capstone Press)

Virginia Plants and Animals. Karla Smith (Heinemann)

Web Sites

Arlington National Cemetery
www.arlingtoncemetery.org/index.htm

Chincoteague Island
www.chincoteague.com/

Colonial Williamsburg
www.history.org/

Virginia State Symbols and Emblems
legis.state.va.us/CapitolClassroom/9-12/9-12Emblems.html